NATIONAL GEOGRAPHIC
WASHINGTON, D.C.

How to Play Funny Fill-In!

Love to create amazing stories? Good, because this one stars YOU. Get ready to laugh with all your friends—you can play with as many people as you want! Make sure to keep this book on your shelf. You'll want to read it again and again!

Are You Ready to Laugh?

- One person picks a story—you can start at the beginning, the middle, or the end of the book.
- Ask a friend to call out a word that the space asks for—noun, verb, or something else—and write it in the blank space. If there's more than one player, ask the next person to say a word. Extra points for creativity!
- When all the spaces are filled in, you have your very own Funny Fill-In. Read it out loud for a laugh.
- Want to play by yourself? Just fold over the page and use the cardboard insert at the back as a writing pad. Fill in the blank parts of speech list, and copy your answers into the story.

Make sure you check out the amazing **Fun Facts** that appear on every page!

Parts of Speech

To play the game, you'll need to know how to form sentences. This list with examples of the parts of speech and other terms will help you get started:

Noun: The name of a person, place, thing, or idea
Examples: tree, mouth, creature
*The **ocean** is full of colorful **fish**.*

Adjective: A word that describes a noun or pronoun
Examples: green, lazy, friendly
*My **silly** dog won't stop laughing!*

Verb: An action word. In the present tense, a verb often ends in –s or –ing. If the space asks for past tense, changing the vowel or adding a –d or –ed to the end usually will set the sentence in the past.
Examples: swim, hide, plays, running (present tense); biked, rode, jumped (past tense)
*The giraffe **skips** across the savanna.*
*The flower **opened** after the rain.*

Adverb: A word that describes a verb and usually ends in –ly
Examples: quickly, lazily, soundlessly
*Kelley **greedily** ate all the carrots.*

Plural: More than one
Examples: mice, telephones, wrenches
*Why are all the **doors** closing?*

Silly Word or Exclamation: A funny sound, a made-up word, a word you think is totally weird, or a noise someone or something might make
Examples: Ouch! No way! Foozleduzzle! Yikes!
*"**Darn!**" shouted Jim. "These cupcakes are sour!"*

Specific Words: There are many more ways to make your story hilarious. When asked for something like a number, animal, or body part, write in something you think is especially funny.

adjective

type of vehicle

friend's name

verb ending in –ing

your age

noun

noun

noun, plural

number

type of food

feeling

number

body part

large number

type of liquid

noun

family member

type of building

adjective

Fun Fact! More than 250 million visitors enjoy America's national parks each year.

Today is going to be ______ (adjective)! We've just finished loading the family ______ (type of vehicle) for our trip to the National Mall and Memorial Parks in Washington, D.C. My family is letting ______ (friend's name), who is better at ______ (verb ending in –ing) than anyone else I know, come along. After what seems like ______ (your age) hours, we're all packed up and ready to go. I've brought along my ______ (noun), a(n) ______ (noun), and ______ (noun, plural) for the ______ (number)-hour drive. We've also packed ______ (type of food) for snacks in case we get ______ (feeling). But after ______ (number) minutes, all the snacks are gone, and my ______ (body part) is sore from sitting on it for so long. We've sung "______ (large number) Bottles of ______ (type of liquid) on the ______ (noun)" so many times that my ______ (family member) has bet us that we can't be quiet until we pass the next ______ (type of building). I bet we can, so I take out the park brochure to read. Inside, it says, "Hey, Kids! Enter our video contest to win an awesome National Parks trip!" What a(n) ______ (adjective) idea!

VIDEO contest

friend's name

verb

feeling

adjective

clothing item, plural

verb

type of animal

large number

type of reptile

adjective

adjective

adjective

type of vehicle, plural

adjective

noun

adjective

Fun Fact! Also known as "America's Front Yard," the National Mall is the most visited area of the National Park System.

The National Mall and Memorial Parks

When we finally get to Washington, D.C., ____________ (friend's name) and I ____________ (verb) and kiss the ground. We're so ____________ (feeling) to finally be here! The first thing we do is strap our ____________ (adjective) cameras onto our ____________ (clothing item, plural). We want to win this video contest. We ____________ (verb) to the Jefferson Memorial to meet up with the park ranger who will be leading us on a bike tour. We set off, and the park ranger takes us to the Franklin Delano Roosevelt Memorial, where I see a statue of the president with his pet ____________ (type of animal), who went with him everywhere! The ranger tells us that many presidents had pets at the White House: Washington had ____________ (large number) hound dogs, Adams had a(n) ____________ (type of reptile) stay with him for a while, Jefferson had a pair of ____________ (adjective) grizzly cubs, and Coolidge even had a(n) ____________ (adjective) pygmy hippo! After the ____________ (adjective) bike tour, we get into paddle ____________ (type of vehicle, plural) to cruise across the Tidal Basin. On the way, I see a(n) ____________ (adjective) ____________ (noun) floating in the water that someone must have dropped, so I pick it up. What a great day! As we leave the park, we drop off our ____________ (adjective) video and hope for the best!

adjective

family member

electronic gadget

noise

friend's name

number

name of a state

name of a state

mythical place

verb ending in –ing

verb ending in –ing

noun, plural

type of food, plural

clothing item, plural

verb

adjective

feeling

type of insect, plural

verb ending in –ing

Fun Fact! When the National Park Service began in 1916, there were 35 national parks and monuments. Today, there are more than 400 designated areas.

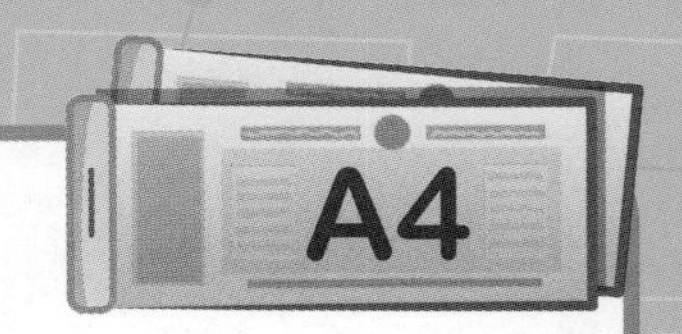

We're on our way home after a(n) ____________ (adjective) day, when suddenly my ____________ (family member)'s ____________ (electronic gadget) makes a loud ____________ (noise)! Good news! ____________ (friend's name) and I won the video contest! ____________ (number) judges from ____________ (name of a state), ____________ (name of a state), and ____________ (mythical place) said that our video was selected because it showed how a park can both educate people and be used for fun things like ____________ (verb ending in -ing) and ____________ (verb ending in -ing). And by picking up ____________ (noun, plural) that didn't belong in the Tidal Basin, we were protecting the park. There's no time to go home and stock up on more ____________ (type of food, plural) and clean ____________ (clothing item, plural) before our plane leaves, so we ____________ (verb) to the nearest airport. There we're met by a(n) ____________ (adjective) park ranger, who will be going with us to all the parks. The ranger looks ____________ (feeling) when we ask if we can sing "The ____________ (type of insect, plural) Go ____________ (verb ending in -ing)" all the way there. Get ready for the trip of a lifetime!

verb

adjective ending in –est

number

feeling

friend's name

body part

verb

large number

verb ending in –ing

type of vehicle

noun

verb ending in –s

famous basketball player

exclamation

number

Fun Fact! American bison weigh up to 2,000 pounds (907 kg), yet they can jump up to six feet (1.8 m) into the air!

Yellowstone National Park

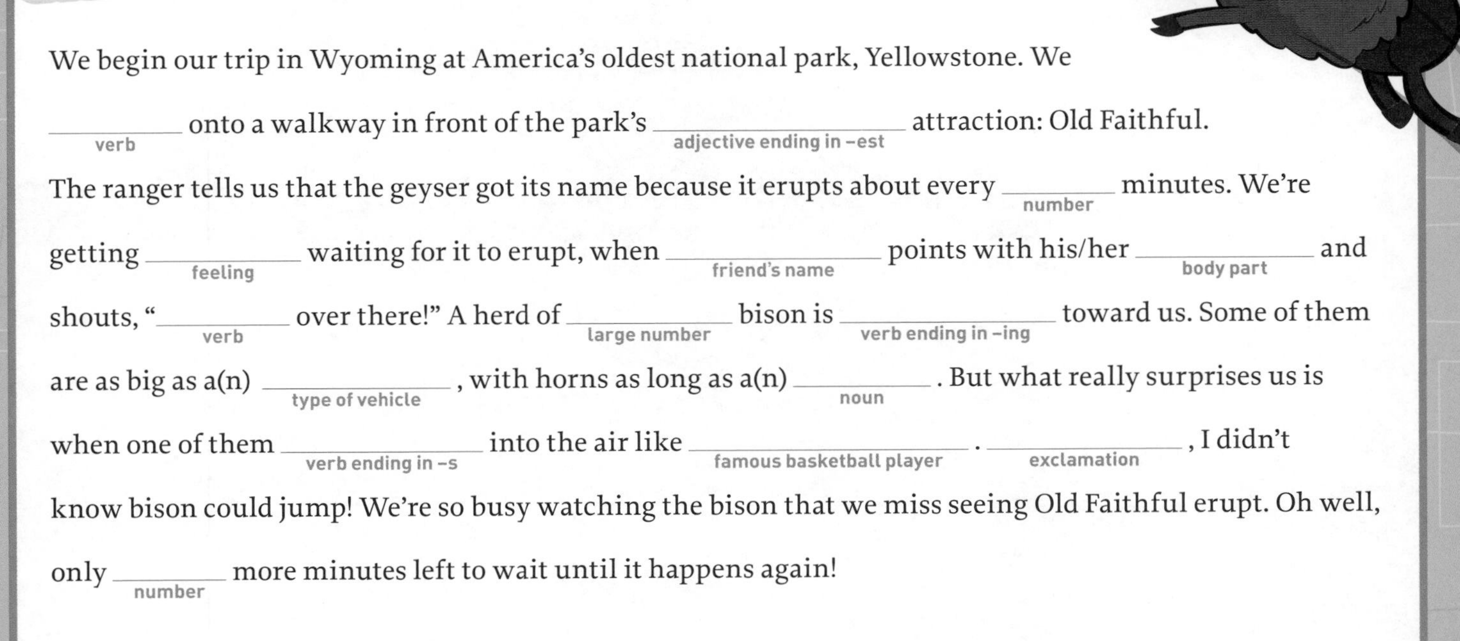

We begin our trip in Wyoming at America's oldest national park, Yellowstone. We ______ (verb) onto a walkway in front of the park's ______ (adjective ending in –est) attraction: Old Faithful. The ranger tells us that the geyser got its name because it erupts about every ______ (number) minutes. We're getting ______ (feeling) waiting for it to erupt, when ______ (friend's name) points with his/her ______ (body part) and shouts, "______ (verb) over there!" A herd of ______ (large number) bison is ______ (verb ending in –ing) toward us. Some of them are as big as a(n) ______ (type of vehicle), with horns as long as a(n) ______ (noun). But what really surprises us is when one of them ______ (verb ending in –s) into the air like ______ (famous basketball player). ______ (exclamation), I didn't know bison could jump! We're so busy watching the bison that we miss seeing Old Faithful erupt. Oh well, only ______ (number) more minutes left to wait until it happens again!

friend's name

body part, plural

verb ending in –ing

clothing item, plural

noun, plural

adjective

verb

adjective

verb ending in –s

body part

large number

verb

verb

verb

adjective

noun, plural

adverb ending in –ly

body part

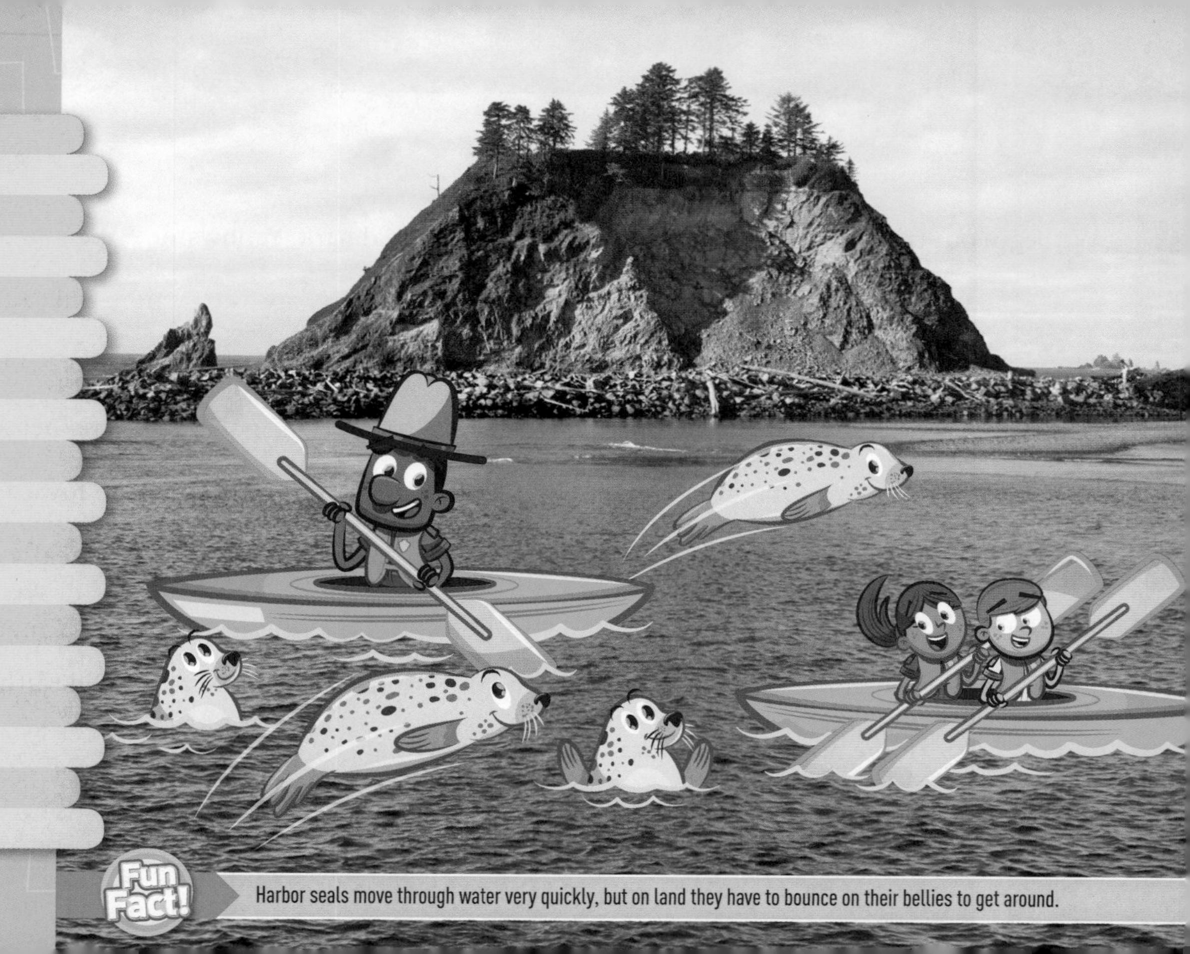

Fun Fact!

Harbor seals move through water very quickly, but on land they have to bounce on their bellies to get around.

Olympic National Park

Next we fly off to the Pacific coast to visit Olympic National Park in Washingston State. ______ (friend's name) and I can't wait to dip our ______ (body part, plural) into the ocean. When we get to the coast, we see people ______ (verb ending in –ing) through the waves on kayaks. So we put on our ______ (clothing item, plural), grab our ______ (noun, plural), and join them. We're paddling around a(n) ______ (adjective) rock when I look into the water and see something ______ (verb) past in the water below. It's a(n) ______ (adjective) harbor seal. It ______ (verb ending in –s) and rolls around in the water. Then it flaps its ______ (body part) at me, and I get soaked! Suddenly I'm surrounded by ______ (large number) seals that ______ (verb) and ______ (verb) through the water. We finish kayaking for the day, and as we ______ (verb) along the coast we see ______ (adjective) seals lying on the ______ (noun, plural). They aren't moving too ______ (adverb ending in –ly) now that they're on land, but I think I see one of them wave its ______ (body part) at me.

verb

name beginning with *R*

name of a fictional character

clothing item, plural

type of plant, plural

adjective

verb

something slimy

your age

verb

noun, plural

color

number

verb

type of fruit

noun

Fun Fact! There are two areas of temperate rain forests in the U.S.—along the Pacific coast and in the southern Appalachians.

We're hiking through Olympic National Park when I ________ (verb) into a hole and an Olympic marmot pops out! We follow it to Hoh Rain Forest, where we see a sign that says "Ranger ________ (name beginning with *R*)'s Rain Forest Race." A ranger who looks like ________ (name of a fictional character) gives us ________ (clothing item, plural) made out of ________ (type of plant, plural) with our race numbers on them. All we have to do to win is finish first in a(n) ________ (adjective) obstacle course along the Hoh River Trail. The race begins, and I try to ________ (verb) across a fallen log to get over a puddle. But the log is coated in ________ (something slimy), and I fall off ________ (your age) times before I make it. Next I have to ________ (verb) up a slope carrying heavy ________ (noun, plural), but the ground is covered in ________ (color) moss, so I slip ________ (number) times before making it to the top. I seem to have fallen behind, so I ________ (verb) around some hemlock trees, looking for everyone. When I finally catch up to them, a(n) ________ (type of fruit) slug is getting the first-place ________ (noun)!

verb

noun, plural

clothing item, plural

type of food

kitchen appliance

noun

favorite video game

adjective

verb

verb

noun

noun

verb ending in –ing

verb

period of time

adjective

noun

type of food

Denali National Park's only amphibian is the tiny wood frog. It freezes solid in winter and then thaws in spring.

Next we head way up north to Denali National Park and Preserve in Alaska—home to North America's tallest mountain. And I want to ________ (verb) it! We join an expedition and buy supplies: waterproof ________ (noun, plural), warm ________ (clothing item, plural), dehydrated ________ (type of food), a gas ________ (kitchen appliance), and a fleece ________ (noun). The park ranger says we'll be on the mountain for several days. That's a long time without ________ (favorite video game). Day 1: Long climb, but what a(n) ________ (adjective) view! Day 2: ________ (verb) up the mountain all day. Spot a golden eagle! Day 3: ________ (verb) around, then build a rock ________ (noun)! Days 4 and 5: Trapped in a(n) ________ (noun) by a snowstorm. Day 6: ________ (verb ending in -ing). Day 7: We ________ (verb) for a(n) ________ (period of time). Day 8: I miss my warm, ________ (adjective) ________ (noun). Day 9: I smell like ________ (type of food). Day 10: We haven't gotten very far—I can still see where we started from!

name of a planet

electronic gadget

adjective

name of a hero

silly word

same silly word

your age

adjective

verb

clothing item, plural

adjective

adjective

verb

verb

type of game

color

noun

Thanks to webcams set up in national parks, you can watch the dog kennels at Denali from your own computer.

We're sitting in Denali, wondering what on ______________ (name of a planet) we're going to do next, when the park ranger pulls out his ______________ (electronic gadget). "I have a(n) ______________ (adjective) idea," he says. A few minutes later, we see something in the distance. Is that ______________ (name of a hero) coming to save us? "______________ (silly word), ______________ (same silly word)," we hear. Then a team of ______________ (your age) dogs and another park ranger on a sled appear. It's a(n) ______________ (adjective) dogsled team. The second ranger tells us to ______________ (verb) on the sled and wrap up in furry ______________ (clothing item, plural) to keep warm. The wind has really started to howl now, and the snow is getting ______________ (adjective). Luckily, the ______________ (adjective) dogs seem to know the way, because when the snow stops, we're parked out front of a patrol station. The dogs get fed, and then they lie down to ______________ (verb) for a little while. After a short rest, they're up again and ready to ______________ (verb), so we take turns playing ______________ (type of game). My favorite dog is the one with the ______________ (color) eyes. And I think she likes me, too, because she gives me a big wet ______________ (noun).

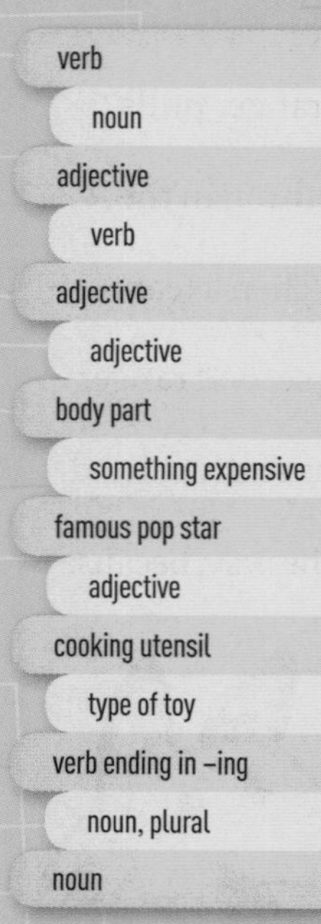

Fun Fact! Cadillac Mountain in Acadia National Park is the highest point along the East Coast of the United States.

Acadia National Park

From Alaska, we ________ (verb) all the way to the Atlantic coast to visit Acadia National Park's Mount Desert Island in Maine. When we get to the park's ________ (noun), the park ranger tells us we're going to have a(n) ________ (adjective) time today, because we get to ________ (verb) around the islands in a sailboat, exploring the coast. Near Baker Island, I see something ________ (adjective) in the water. It's a harbor porpoise! It has something ________ (adjective) on its ________ (body part). Is that a(n) ________ (something expensive) like ________ (famous pop star) wears? Then I see a(n) ________ (adjective) whale float by with a(n) ________ (cooking utensil). But things get really strange when a dolphin swims by with a(n) ________ (type of toy). That's when the park ranger explains that there are shipwrecks in these waters. These animals must have been ________ (verb ending in -ing) for treasure at a wreck. I wonder if there are any golden ________ (noun, plural) or a priceless ________ (noun) on the seabed just waiting to be discovered!

adjective

verb

adjective

animal noise

noun

verb

adjective

body part

verb ending in –s

body part

friend's name

animal noise

verb

verb ending in –s

number

adjective

body part

adjective

Fun Fact! An anhinga can swim through the water with only its neck above the surface—making it look like an upright swimming snake!

Everglades National Park

For our next stop, we head as far down the coast as we can, to Everglades National Park in ________ (adjective) Florida. There, we ________ (verb) along a trail to a boardwalk over a(n) ________ (adjective) marsh. Tons of birds ________ (animal noise) and dart across the sky. One of them lands on a(n) ________ (noun) right in front of me. My friend pulls out his/her camera. I see a wood stork and pretend to ________ (verb) like it, keeping my legs ________ (adjective) and hunching my ________ (body part). A common yellowthroat ________ (verb ending in –s) its song, and I puff out my ________ (body part) and copy it in a funny voice. This makes ________ (friend's name) ________ (animal noise) and almost ________ (verb) into the marsh. Unfortunately, the camera goes flying into the water before I can grab it. To our surprise, an anhinga bird ________ (verb ending in –s) in after it. ________ (number) second(s) later, it reappears with the camera hanging around its ________ (adjective) ________ (body part)! How ________ (adjective)!

noun, plural

type of bird

adjective

adjective

type of animal

type of animal

friend's name

cartoon character

noun

type of animal, plural

verb

verb

noun

large number

Fun Fact!

Red mangroves are sometimes called "walking trees," because their propped roots make them look like they are walking on water.

Mangroves and Manatees

Wanting to see more of the Everglades, we rent boats shaped like ________ (noun, plural) from the ________ (type of bird) Marina. The first thing we see when we get out onto the water is a manatee! The park ranger tells us how ________ (adjective) we are to see one, since they are very ________ (adjective). I think it looks like a(n) ________ (type of animal) crossed with a(n) ________ (type of animal), but ________ (friend's name) thinks it looks just like ________ (cartoon character). Soon we pass by the manatee, since it's only moving as fast as a floating ________ (noun), and enter into a red mangrove forest. Here there are trees that look like they are growing right out of the water, with roots shaped like crawling ________ (type of animal, plural). "Let's play hide-and-________ (verb) among the trees," I say. But then the park ranger tells us to ________ (verb) at a log in the water. Suddenly, we're looking into a mouth as wide as a(n) ________ (noun), with ________ (large number) teeth. *Gulp!* An alligator! I think we'll just stay in the boat ...

type of building

verb

adjective

dance move

silly word

friend's name

noun

body part

adjective

color

verb ending in –ing

noun

your age

verb

verb ending in –ing

noun

gymnastics move

name of a game

Fun Fact! It is illegal to come within 50 yards (46 m)—about half the length of a football field—of a black bear in the park.

Great Smoky Mountains National Park

For our next adventure, we're going hiking in North Carolina and Tennessee's Great Smoky Mountains National Park. After we pick up our permits from the ranger ____________ (type of building), we start to ____________ (verb) along a narrow path. Just as I'm thinking about what a(n) ____________ (adjective) place this is, the ranger suddenly does a(n) ____________ (dance move) and yells out, "Hey, ____________ (silly word)!" ____________ (friend's name) and I stop and look at the ranger like he has a(n) ____________ (noun) on his ____________ (body part). Then the ranger points into the woods. We see a(n) ____________ (adjective) ____________ (color) body part poking out from behind a tree. "Shhhh. Bears," the ranger whispers. "If we stay really still and don't make any noise, we'll be able to see them ____________ (verb ending in –ing)." We stay as still as a(n) ____________ (noun) for ____________ (your age) minutes, but we don't see any more sign of the bears. We decide to ____________ (verb) on down the path. Just as we turn a bend, we see them! One bear is ____________ (verb ending in –ing) on a(n) ____________ (noun), while another does a(n) ____________ (gymnastics move). Two more look like they're playing ____________ (name of a game)! It looks like so much fun, I wish we could play, too!

noise

same noise

type of vehicle

body part

verb

adjective

adjective

noun, plural

noun, plural

color

type of tool, plural

type of profession, plural

type of utensil, plural

adjective

verb

day of the week

verb ending in –ed

type of animal, plural

Fun Fact! The Great Smoky Mountains get their name from the fog or mist that settles in the area after summer rainstorms.

Blast From the Past

We're walking along a trail in the Great Smokies when we hear a(n) ________ (noise) - ________ (same noise) sound.
A tour ________ (type of vehicle) pulls up beside us, and a woman pokes her ________ (body part) out the window. "Do
you want to ________ (verb) along with us?" she asks. "We're going to visit a(n) ________ (adjective) pioneer village."
We climb aboard. The first building we come to has a(n) ________ (adjective) waterwheel. "This is where the
pioneers ground up ________ (noun, plural) to make ________ (noun, plural)," the guide tells us. Next stop is the
________ (color) -smith shop, where ________ (type of tool, plural) for the ________ (type of profession, plural) and the ________ (type of utensil, plural)
for the pioneers were made. We also pass a(n) ________ (adjective) church where the people
met to ________ (verb) every ________ (day of the week), and the log homes where they ________ (verb ending in –ed).
But the coolest part for me was the place where they kept their ________ (type of animal, plural).

adjective ending in –er

body part

clothing item, plural

body part

same body part, plural

verb ending in –s

adverb ending in –ly

adjective

type of animal

your name

adjective

friend's name

body part

verb ending in –s

Fun Fact! In summer, a ptarmigan's feathers are brown and white to blend in with rocks; in winter they are white to blend in with the snow.

Rocky Mountain National Park

It sure is ______________ (adjective ending in -er) at our next stop. That's because we're way up in the mountains of Rocky Mountain National Park in Colorado and surrounded by snow as deep as my ______________ (body part)! We're just about to strap on our snow-______________ (clothing item, plural) and go for a walk when we see a large ______________ (body part) poking out of the snow. I'd recognize ______________ (same body part, plural) like that anywhere—a snowshoe hare. It ______________ (verb ending in -s) away, and we follow it ______________ (adverb ending in -ly) until we come to a clearing. Wow! Whoever was here before us made some really ______________ (adjective) snow sculptures. There is a hare, a pika, an elk, and even a(n) ______________ (type of animal)—all made of snow! I decide to make a snow ______________ (your name) with a really ______________ (adjective) nose. ______________ (friend's name) makes one with a great big ______________ (body part). But I think first prize should go to a white-tailed ptarmigan—until it suddenly ______________ (verb ending in -s) away!

type of animal, plural

verb

adjective

verb

color

verb

noun

noun

body part, plural

adjective ending in –er

friend's name

name of a pop star

verb

adjective

feeling

body part

number

feeling

verb

Fun Fact! In 1881, a tunnel was drilled through a giant sequoia tree in Yosemite. Cars could drive right through the tree!

Yosemite National Park

Next stop: Yosemite National Park in California. As soon as we arrive, we rent ____________ (type of animal, plural) and ____________ (verb) through the park. At Mariposa Grove, we see ____________ (adjective) sequoia trees that are so huge a car could ____________ (verb) right through them! Above us ____________ (color) squirrels ____________ (verb) and jump from branch to ____________ (noun). I drop my backpack onto a(n) ____________ (noun) and get right up close to one of the trees. I try to wrap my ____________ (body part, plural) around the trunk, but I would need to be ____________ (adjective ending in –er) to reach! When I see ____________ (friend's name) posing like ____________ (name of a pop star), I ____________ (verb) and reach for my backpack to get my ____________ (adjective) camera. But my backpack is missing! The park ranger looks ____________ (feeling). He shakes his ____________ (body part) and says, "Rule number ____________ (number): Never leave your backpack unattended. But don't be ____________ (feeling), I have some friends who might be able to help." So off we ____________ (verb) to find the ranger's friends.

verb

adjective

number

type of building, plural

adjective

adjective ending in –est

verb ending in –ing

adjective

noun, plural

adverb ending in –ly

verb ending in –ing

number

type of animal

verb ending in –s

number

color

Fun Fact! Bridalveil Fall in Yosemite National Park got its name because when the wind blows, the water blows sideways, resembling a bride's veil .

We ______ (verb) behind the park ranger until we come to an area where there are ______ (adjective) rock cliffs that are ______ (number) times taller than the ______ (type of building, plural) at home. We hear ______ (adjective) roaring and smashing sounds. It's Yosemite Falls, the ______ (adjective ending in -est) waterfall in the country! "Oh, good! My friends are here," says the park ranger. We start ______ (verb ending in -ing) over to ask some ______ (adjective)-looking people sitting on ______ (noun, plural) outside a lodge, but instead the park ranger stops very ______ (adverb ending in -ly). In front of us ______ (verb ending in -ing) on the grass are ______ (number) mule deer. They have ears like a(n) ______ (type of animal). "Shhh," whispers the park ranger, and he starts moving his ears up and down. Then one of the mule deer moves its ears, too! The park ranger nods in thanks and ______ (verb ending in -s) over to a fallen log. Inside we find ______ (number) ______ (color) squirrels, and they have my backpack!

adjective

type of food

adjective

large number

type of liquid

verb

friend's name

verb

noun, plural

verb

verb ending in –ing

noun

exclamation

color

color

same friend's name

silly word

name of a planet

verb

Fun Fact! "Alien," or invasive, species can be harmful to the plants and animals found in the parks naturally.

Death Valley National Park

Now that I have my backpack again, we move on to our next stop on the trip: Death Valley National Park in California and Nevada. It's so ________ (adjective) in this desert that we could probably cook a(n) ________ (type of food) on the sand! I'm so ________ (adjective) I could drink ________ (large number) glasses of ________ (type of liquid). We ________ (verb) over to Badwater Basin, where we see a pool of water. ________ (friend's name) and I quickly ________ (verb) to the ground to fill our ________ (noun, plural). "________ (verb)!" shouts the park ranger. "Drinking that will make you feel like a(n) ________ (verb ending in –ing) ________ (noun)." So instead we head to Dante's View to watch the sun set over the salt flats and the sand dunes. "________ (exclamation)! Are we still on Earth?" I ask when I see the sky turn ________ (color) and ________ (color) above the cliffs. ________ (same friend's name) jokes, "My name is ________ (silly word)-lexor. Welcome to ________ (name of a planet)." Just then we see something ________ (verb) and flash across the sky. Could it be ... ?

silly word

your teacher's name

famous explorer

name of a country

verb ending in -s

verb

animal sound

friend's name

verb

something gross

noun

body part

verb

same noun

color

boy's name

your town

Fun Fact! Death Valley is home to Furnace Creek, the hottest and driest place in North America.

Gecko the Guardian

When the park ranger asks us if we want to stargaze at night in Death Valley, we say "________ (silly word)" right away! There are so many stars here that we can even see the ________ (your teacher's name) galaxy. I'm lying on the ground, dreaming that I'm ________ (famous explorer) exploring ________ (name of a country), when suddenly a bat ________ (verb ending in -s) overhead and I nearly ________ (verb) out of my skin. Next, a spooky ________ (animal sound) echoes all around us. Coyotes! ________ (friend's name) and I ________ (verb) in fear! Then we smell ________ (something gross). It's a spotted skunk! I'm about to grab a(n) ________ (noun) for protection, when a desert banded gecko runs up my ________ (body part). I ________ (verb) when I see a black widow spider on the ________ (same noun)—that gecko saved my life! When we finally get back to our lodge for the night, I notice that the gecko has followed us. So we invite it in, and we settle back to watch the old Western playing on TV. ________ (color) ________ (boy's name) *and the* ________ (your town) *Heist*—my favorite!

verb

adjective

adjective

adjective

verb ending in –s

fast-moving animal

verb ending in –ing

name of a superhero

adjective

adjective

verb ending in –s

exclamation

Fun Fact! Thanks to conservation efforts of park rangers, the nēnē goose, Hawaii's endangered state bird, was brought back from the brink of extinction.

Hawai'i Volcanoes National Park

The next day, we arrive at Hawai'i Volcanoes National Park. We're going to ______ (verb) around Kilauea, one of the ______ (adjective) volcanoes that created the Hawaiian Islands. The park ranger tells us that Kilauea is one of the most active and ______ (adjective) volcanoes in the world. We're driving down the road when suddenly the ______ (adjective) ranger slams on the brakes. He ______ (verb ending in -s) out the door and takes off like a(n) ______ (fast-moving animal)! "It's a nēnē goose," the park ranger says, escorting the bird off the road. "It's Hawaii's state bird, and it's endangered." The park ranger is just about to tell us what we'll see at Kilauea, but then he takes off again! He's ______ (verb ending in -ing) like ______ (name of a superhero). He takes a(n) ______ (adjective) leap and lands in front of a(n) ______ (adjective) turtle. "Endangered hawksbill turtle!" the ranger gasps. We watch as the turtle ______ (verb ending in -s) across the road. ______ (exclamation)! These rangers take their job seriously!

number

noun

color

adjective

number

verb

color

type of dinosaur

type of liquid

verb

body part

adjective ending in –est

color

adjective

noise

Fun Fact! Kilauea is the world's most active volcano. It produces so much lava, it's added about 500 acres (202 ha) of land to the Big Island since 1983!

After rescuing ______ (number) animal(s), we finally set out on our tour of the volcano. At the first stop, we look out over a crater as big as a(n) ______ (noun) with ______ (color) dried lava everywhere. ______ (adjective) clouds of steam seep up from below ground. It must be ______ (number) degree(s) under the surface to make this much steam. We ______ (verb) down a path with ______ (color) ferns growing on either side. This place looks like a prehistoric jungle—I wonder if a(n) ______ (type of dinosaur) will appear! Then, suddenly, it starts to pour down ______ (type of liquid).

"______ (verb) for it!" the ranger shouts, and we all take off down the path to the ______ (body part) of a cave. When we step inside, we see the ______ (adjective ending in –est) thing ever: The walls are coated with ______ (color) lava! The ranger tells us that this is a lava tube. It was made when ______ (adjective) lava flowed underneath Earth's surface. We hear a loud ______ (noise) from outside the lava tube. Was that thunder, or a volcanic eruption? Or maybe even a dinosaur?

your favorite sport

verb ending in –ing

name of a place

clothing item

adjective

adjective

verb ending in –ed

silly word

adjective

noun

girl's name

boy's name

same girl's name

type of vegetable

your favorite treat

verb ending in –s

verb

friend's name

Fun Fact! The Grand Canyon's California condor is the largest land bird in North America, with a wingspan of nine feet (2.7 m).

Grand Canyon National Park

Whitewater rafting in Grand Canyon National Park, Arizona, is our last stop on the trip. It's more fun than ______________ (your favorite sport) and just a little less scary than ______________ (verb ending in -ing) in ______________ (name of a place) wearing only a(n) ______________ (clothing item). I'm soaked, but it's ______________ (adjective) out and I feel ______________ (adjective). When our raft is ______________ (verb ending in -ed) into the air by a wave, I hear someone yell "______________ (silly word)!" After rafting, we head to ______________ (adjective) ______________ (noun) Lodge. There, we meet ______________ (girl's name) and ______________ (boy's name)—the two mules taking us down into the canyon. But when we try to start out, ______________ (same girl's name) sits down and won't move! We offer her a(n) ______________ (type of vegetable). Nope. Then we offer her ______________ (your favorite treat), and she ______________ (verb ending in -s)! We start to ______________ (verb) down the trail. The view is amazing. I try to take a selfie, but ______________ (friend's name) and his/her mule keep photobombing me!

verb

body part, plural

type of liquid

type of food

your favorite song

adjective

feeling

noise

body part, plural

number

noun, plural

type of food

verb

nickname, plural

something sparkly, plural

adjective

clothing item

friend's name

number

Fun Fact! The National Park System's Junior Ranger program allows you to be sworn in as a Junior Ranger and receive a badge and certificate.

We arrive at a ranch and __________ (verb) off our mules. Oh, my aching __________ (body part, plural)! The ranger tells us to lead our mules behind the building to get them some __________ (type of liquid) and __________ (type of food). But my mule won't budge until I sing "__________ (your favorite song)" to her in a(n) __________ (adjective) voice. I'm pretty darn __________ (feeling) by the time I get around back. But then I hear a loud __________ (noise) and clapping of __________ (body part, plural). A video screen is set up and __________ (number) park ranger(s) are sitting on __________ (noun, plural) with buckets of __________ (type of food). "__________ (verb) down over here, __________ (nickname, plural)," a park ranger says. "You're the __________ (something sparkly, plural) of the show." She reaches over and takes my __________ (adjective) camera off of my __________ (clothing item). "You've been wearing this the whole time, and we saw it all on a live feed! Congratulations! You've just won a trip to tour more of our national parks!" __________ (friend's name) and I high-__________ (number)! Let's go again!

Credits

Cover: RIRF Stock/Shutterstock; 4, Blaz Kure/Shutterstock, Annaev/Shutterstock; 6, Orhan Cam/Shutterstock; 8, Wang Song/Shutterstock; 10, Oleksandr Koretskyi/Shutterstock; 12, Galyna Andrushko/Shutterstock; 14, D. Kroner/Shutterstock; 16, Tom Roche/Shutterstock; 18, Claude Huot/Shutterstock; 20, Joseph Sohm/Shutterstock; 22, Ivan Cholakov/Shutterstock; 24, Jeremy What/Shutterstock; 26, Jon Bilous/Shutterstock; 28, Jon Bilous/Shutterstock; 30, Dr. Alan Lipkin/Shutterstock; 32, Turtix/Shutterstock; 34, Phent/Shutterstock; 36, Telesniuk/Shutterstock; 38, Tobkatrina/Shutterstock; 40, Nickolay Stanev/Shutterstock; 42, Radoslaw Lecyk/Shutterstock; 44, Oleksandr Koretskyi/Shutterstock; 46, Gary Whitton/Shutterstock

Staff for This Book
Ariane Szu-Tu, *Project Editor*
Callie Broaddus, *Art Director*
Kelley Miller, *Senior Photo Editor*
Jeff Heimsath, *Photo Editor*
Jennifer MacKinnon, *Writer*
Jason Tharp, *Illustrator*
Paige Towler, *Editorial Assistant*
Rachel Kenny and Sanjida Rashid, *Design Production Assistants*
Tammi Colleary-Loach, *Rights Clearance Manager*
Mari Robinson and Michael Cassady, *Rights Clearance Specialists*
Grace Hill, *Managing Editor*
Alix Inchausti, *Production Editor*
Lewis R. Bassford, *Production Manager*
Jenn Hoff, *Manager, Production Services*
Susan Borke, *Legal and Business Affairs*

Published by the National Geographic Society
Gary E. Knell, *President and CEO*
John M. Fahey, *Chairman of the Board*
Melina Gerosa Bellows, *Chief Education Officer*
Declan Moore, *Chief Media Officer*
Hector Sierra, *Senior Vice President and General Manager, Book Division*

Senior Management Team, Kids Publishing and Media
Nancy Laties Feresten, *Senior Vice President*
Jennifer Emmett, *Vice President, Editorial Director, Kids Books*
Julie Vosburgh Agnone, *Vice President, Editorial Operations*
Rachel Buchholz, *Editor and Vice President,* NG Kids *magazine*
Michelle Sullivan, *Vice President, Kids Digital*
Eva Absher-Schantz, *Design Director*
Jay Sumner, *Photo Director*
Hannah August, *Marketing Director*
R. Gary Colbert, *Production Director*

Digital
Laura Goertzel, *Manager*
Sara Zeglin, *Senior Producer*
Bianca Bowman, *Assistant Producer*
Natalie Jones, *Senior Product Manager*

Editorial, Design, and Production by Plan B Book Packagers

The publisher gratefully acknowledges the National Park Service for their review of this book.

For more information about our National Parks, visit natgeo.com/kids/parks.

The National Geographic Society is one of the world's largest nonprofit scientific and educational organizations. Founded in 1888 to "increase and diffuse geographic knowledge," the Society's mission is to inspire people to care about the planet. It reaches more than 400 million people worldwide each month through its official journal, *National Geographic*, and other magazines; National Geographic Channel; television documentaries; music; radio; films; books; DVDs; maps; exhibitions; live events; school publishing programs; interactive media; and merchandise. National Geographic has funded more than 10,000 scientific research, conservation, and exploration projects and supports an education program promoting geographic literacy.

For more information, please visit nationalgeographic.com, call 1-800-NGS LINE (647-5463), or write to the following address:

National Geographic Society, 1145 17th Street N.W., Washington, D.C. 20036-4688 U.S.A.

Visit us online at nationalgeographic.com/books

For librarians and teachers: ngchildrensbooks.org

More for kids from National Geographic: kids.nationalgeographic.com

For information about special discounts for bulk purchases, please contact National Geographic Books Special Sales: ngspecsales@ngs.org

For rights or permissions inquiries, please contact National Geographic Books Subsidiary Rights: ngbookrights@ngs.org

ISBN: 978-1-4263-2303-4

Printed in China

15/RRDS/1